STEP INTO READING®

STEP 4

VOLCANOES!
Mountains of Fire

By Eric Arnold

Illustrated by Doug Knutson

Random House 🏠 New York

1
Nature's Time Bomb

It is early morning on Sunday, May 18, 1980.
Many people in Washington State are
still asleep. But not the volcano Mount St.
Helens. It is slowly waking up from a deep
sleep of 123 years.

Mount St. Helens is as pretty as a
postcard. The nearby forests and rivers
are rich with birds, fish, deer, and other
wildlife. The area is perfect for hiking and
camping.

Dear Parent:

Congratulations! Your child is taking the first steps on an exciting journey. The destination? Independent reading!

STEP INTO READING® will help your child get there. The program offers five steps to reading success. Each step includes fun stories and colorful art. There are also Step into Reading Sticker Books, Step into Reading Math Readers, Step into Reading Write-In Readers, Step into Reading Phonics Readers, and Step into Reading Phonics First Steps! Boxed Sets—a complete literacy program with something for every child.

Learning to Read, Step by Step!

Ready to Read   Preschool–Kindergarten
• big type and easy words • rhyme and rhythm • picture clues
For children who know the alphabet and are eager to begin reading.

Reading with Help   Preschool–Grade 1
• basic vocabulary • short sentences • simple stories
For children who recognize familiar words and sound out new words with help.

Reading on Your Own   Grades 1–3
• engaging characters • easy-to-follow plots • popular topics
For children who are ready to read on their own.

Reading Paragraphs   Grades 2–3
• challenging vocabulary • short paragraphs • exciting stories
For newly independent readers who read simple sentences with confidence.

Ready for Chapters   Grades 2–4
• chapters • longer paragraphs • full-color art
For children who want to take the plunge into chapter books but still like colorful pictures.

STEP INTO READING® is designed to give every child a successful reading experience. The grade levels are only guides. Children can progress through the steps at their own speed, developing confidence in their reading, no matter what their grade.

Remember, a lifetime love of reading starts with a single step!

In loving memory of my parents,
and for Christen and our Tali and Gabriel—
we have a lava fun!
A special thanks to Mike Rhodes
(Dept. of Geosciences, University of Massachusetts)
for his time and expertise,
to Damien Keith, to Shana Corey,
and to the Cowlitz County Advocate,
Castle Rock, Washington.
Heartfelt thanks to my editor, Heidi Kilgras—
my "Magma, P.I."

Text copyright © 1997 by Eric Arnold. Illustrations copyright © 1997 by Doug Knutson.
All rights reserved under International and Pan-American Copyright Conventions. Published
in the United States by Random House Children's Books, a division of Random House, Inc.,
New York, and simultaneously in Canada by Random House of Canada Limited, Toronto.

www.stepintoreading.com

Educators and librarians, for a variety of teaching tools, visit us at
www.randomhouse.com/teachers

Library of Congress Cataloging-in-Publication Data
Arnold, Eric.
Volcanoes! : mountains of fire / by Eric Arnold ; illustrated by Doug Knutson.
    p.   cm. — (Step into reading. A step 4 book)
Originally published: New York : Random House, c1997, in series: Step into reading. Step 3 book.
SUMMARY: Describes the eruption of Mount St. Helens in Washington state in 1980 and provides
a simple explanation of how and why volcanoes erupt.
ISBN 0-679-88641-9 (trade) — ISBN 0-679-98641-3 (lib. bdg.)
1. Volcanoes—Juvenile literature. [1. Volcanoes.]
I. Knutson, Doug, ill. II. Title. III. Series: Step into reading. Step 4 book.
QE521.3 .A76 2003   551.21—dc21   2002014938

Printed in the United States of America   30 29 28 27 26 25 24 23 22

STEP INTO READING, RANDOM HOUSE, and the Random House colophon are registered trademarks
of Random House, Inc.

People have lived and worked for many years in towns near the volcano. Few of them fear the power of this sleeping giant.

A small plane flies over Mount St. Helens to get a closer look at the volcano. Pilot Bruce Judson sees something happening below. Pieces of rock and ice are sliding into the crater, the hole at the top. He tips the plane to get a better view inside the crater.

Suddenly, an avalanche of rocks rushes down the north side of the mountain. The landslide tears open a hole in the volcano. An explosion of steam, ash, and rock blasts out sideways.

Then, a few seconds later—KABLAM! The top of the volcano blasts off! A dark ash cloud shoots 15 miles into the sky. The ash cloud has tiny bits of rock and gas inside it.

Luckily, the plane is not in the direct path of the cloud. But the cloud is closing in on the plane. Outside the window, the morning turns to total darkness.

Bruce knows he has to get out of there—and fast. He puts the plane into a dive to gain speed.

Lightning bolts streak through the clouds, lighting up the sky. The clouds are heading north, so Bruce quickly steers the plane south. After a few minutes, he outraces them. With a lot of skill and a lot of luck, he lands the plane safely in Portland, Oregon.

2

The Moon on Earth

The dark ash clouds move fast and far. They block the sun and make day look like night. In Yakima (YAK-uh-ma), a town 80 miles northeast of Mount St. Helens, the street lights automatically turn on!

Ash falls like black snow. If people or animals get too much of it in their lungs, they cannot breathe. Ash also ruins motors in cars, trucks, and buses.

A family is camping in a cabin nearby
when the ash clouds pass overhead. Small
rocks start to rain down from the clouds.
The sky becomes pitch black.

Thunder shakes the cabin. Lightning
looks like a flash from a giant camera.
When bits of ash bump into each other in
the clouds, they make static electricity.
This creates bolts of lightning.

The highway outside the cabin is

closed. It is covered with six inches of ash!
Inside, the family huddles together. They
don't think they will get out alive.

For three days, they are trapped in the
cabin. Finally, on the fourth day, it is safe
for them to leave the cabin and head home.

The snow on Mount St. Helens melts from the heat of the blast. It mixes with the fallen ash and forms a river of thick mud called a mudflow. The mudflow buries everything in its path as it rushes into rivers and streams. Houses and cars are swept away as if they were toys!

Mount St. Helens erupts all day. The next day it rests, but much has been destroyed.

After the eruption, the volcano is 1,300 feet shorter. A big, new crater is at the top in the shape of a horseshoe.

Entire forests have been destroyed. Trees as tall as city buildings were knocked down by the powerful sideways blast. The temperature of the blast was hotter than an oven. The trees burned, losing their branches and leaves. They now look like giant toothpicks.

The land around Mount St. Helens looks like the surface of the moon. Most of the wildlife is dead.

And 57 people have lost their lives!

3
Warning!

Volcanologists (scientists who study volcanoes) tried to warn people before the big eruption.

Dave Johnston and several other volcanologists set up an observation post six miles from Mount St. Helens. They had been watching the volcano closely for months because it had started to erupt. So far, the eruptions had been small and harmless.

They also noticed that the volcano was swelling on its north side. This swelling was caused by magma, or melted rock found beneath the earth's surface, moving up into the volcano. It was like a keg of dynamite ready to blast!

Dave knew the power of a volcano. He had seen the eruption of Mount Augustine in Alaska. He warned people who lived near Mount St. Helens that the next eruption might be a big one. Dave didn't know the exact day or time it would blast, or how big it would be. But he wanted people to leave their homes so they would be safe.

Many did. But some people didn't listen.

Harry Truman owned an inn near the volcano. He was 83 years old. He lived there with his 16 cats. Harry was one of the people who refused to leave. He said, "This mountain is my life."

The blast covered his inn with 40 feet of ash. No one ever saw Harry and his cats again.

Dave was on duty when the volcano erupted. The observation post was destroyed. Dave's trailer was blown apart, and his truck was buried in ash.

Dave lost his life to the great power of Mount St. Helens.

4

Fire in the Mountain

Volcanologists look for clues that will help them predict when a volcano will erupt. This is hard to do, because each eruption is different and some happen without warning!

It is dangerous work, but many lives can be saved from what volcanologists discover. The lessons learned from the Mount St. Helens eruption helped scientists to predict the eruption of Mount Pinatubo

(pin-uh-TOO-bo) in the Philippines in 1991. The eruption of Mount Pinatubo was eight times bigger than that of Mount St. Helens.

People were moved to safe places before the eruption happened. Though about 200 people died, thousands of lives were saved.

Much of the work of volcanologists is done in a laboratory, where they look at samples of gas and lava. But they also work right on a volcano. This is called fieldwork. They record the day-to-day life of a volcano.

Volcanologists take a volcano's temperature with a special electric thermometer. (They don't use a glass thermometer, because glass would break from the extreme heat.)

When they want to get close to the "hot" action, volcanologists sometimes wear fireproof suits. The temperature inside the suit stays cool.

Some volcanologists study volcanoes on other planets. Satellites take pictures in outer space, and scientists study them. The biggest volcano in the solar system is Olympus Mons on the planet Mars. It's almost three times the height of Mount Everest!

Volcanologists ride inside *Alvin*, a submarine, to collect samples of volcanic rock.

But not all volcanologists are human! *Dante,* a robot, was built to crawl into the crater of Mount Erebus (AIR-uh-bus) in Antarctica to measure lava and gas.

Here's how a volcano works:

The earth has a layer of "skin" that is made of rock. The earth's skin is called the crust. The crust is like a jigsaw puzzle made up of giant pieces called plates. These plates move very slowly—a few inches a year. Why do they move? Because they sit on top of rock that is very, very hot. The rock gets so hot in spots that it melts.

SMACK!

When the plates bump each other or pull apart, a crack may form in the crust. Magma and gas push up through the crack. Once magma is outside of the volcano, it is called lava.

Sometimes lava explodes in a cloud and shoots out of the crater, as it did in the Mount St. Helens eruption. But some volcanoes don't explode when they erupt.

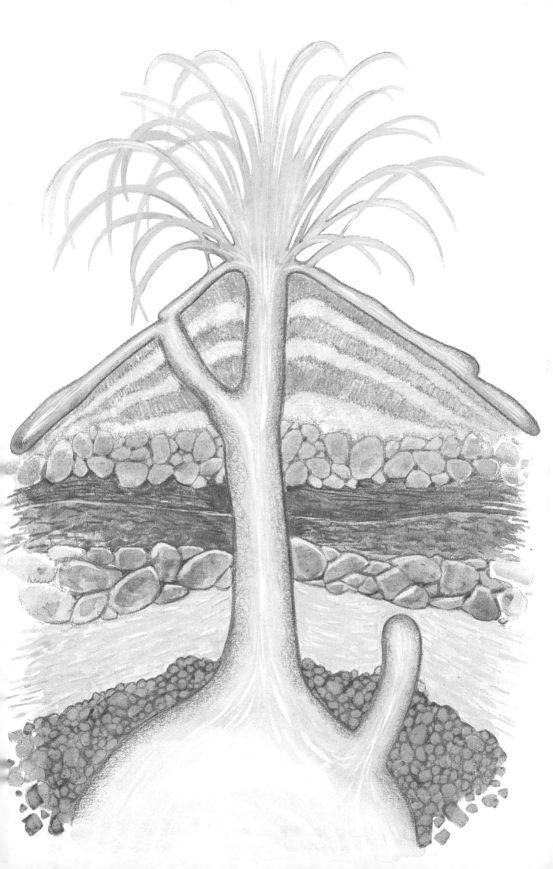

Instead, streams of hot lava flow out. The volcanoes of Hawaii erupt this way. The lava flows are beautiful, but they are like a "river of fire." They burn everything in their path!

A volcano gets bigger from layers of lava and ash building up on its sides.

When magma or lava cools, different types of volcanic, or igneous (IG-nee-us), rock are formed. Granite forms when magma cools slowly in cracks beneath the earth's surface.

Basalt forms when a stream of lava cools quickly. Pumice (PUM-is), the lightest rock in the world, is made when thick, sticky lava cools fast. Pumice hardens with air bubbles inside—it is so light, it can float in water.

5
Yesterday and Today

Two thousand years ago in Italy, a boy saw Mount Vesuvius (vuh-SOO-vee-us) erupt. His name was Pliny (PLIN-ee). Ash from Mount Vesuvius buried the whole town of Pompeii (pom-PAY). Mount Vesuvius had been dormant, or sleeping, for a long time. When it erupted, everything was destroyed. The people who didn't escape in time were buried alive.

People wanted to know what happened at Mt. Vesuvius. Pliny wrote letters describing what an erupting volcano looked like. This made him the world's first volcanologist!

He wrote that the earth shook before the blast. (An earthquake is a signal that a volcano is ready to blow!) Pliny also wrote that a tall cloud shot up in the shape of a pine tree. This kind of blast was named after him. It is called a Plinian (PLIN-ee-un) eruption.

But Pliny could not explain why a volcano erupts. Instead, myths were told to explain it.

In ancient Rome, people believed fire from a volcano came from the blacksmith shop of Vulcan, the god of fire. The word "volcano" comes from his name.

Vulcan was the blacksmith of the gods. In his shop inside a volcano, he made thunderbolts for Jupiter, the king of the gods, and weapons for Mars, the god of war.

In Hawaii, people believed volcanoes erupted because of Pele (PAY-lay), the goddess of fire. Pele had a bad temper. When she got mad, she made volcanoes erupt by digging a "fire pit" in the ground with a magic stick. The other gods chased Pele in her canoe from island to island because she started fires in the mountains. She died in battle, and her spirit now lives in the crater of Kilauea (kee-lou-AY-ah).

Kilauea is an "active" volcano, which means it can erupt at any time. It is one of the most active in the world and is known for its beautiful lava flows. Some say Pele appears when Kilauea erupts. She shows up as a young girl or an old woman. Some see her face in the glow of the blast.

Today, there are between 500 and 600 active volcanoes on earth. Many of these volcanoes circle the shores of the Pacific Ocean. This is called the Ring of Fire.

About 30 volcanoes erupt each year.

Where will the next big eruption take place?

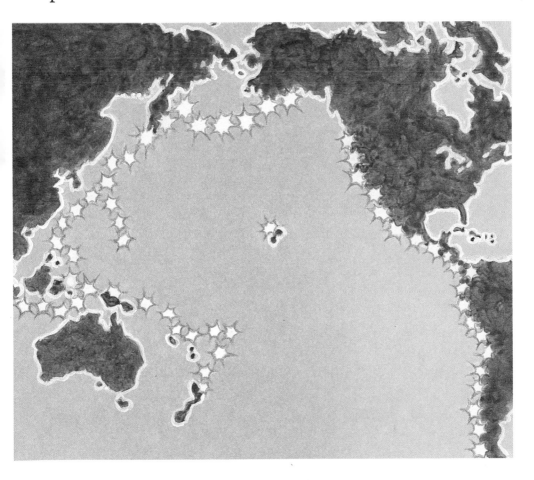

6

Nature Heals

Can life return to land that has been destroyed by a volcanic eruption?

A few months had passed, and Mount St. Helens was now welcoming the warm summer weather. The circle of life was returning to this gray moonscape. Volcanic ash had made the soil rich.

Red fireweed was the first plant to pop up. It grows well in soil burned by fire. Tiny fir trees also took root.

Bluebirds and woodpeckers returned and nested in the dead trees. For mealtime, there were plenty of ladybugs and ants to eat.

Small animals such as gophers came back. Gophers make tunnels that bring good soil to the top.

Herds of elk and deer returned from far away to feed on the new growth on bushes.

And many of the people of Mount St. Helens returned to their homes or built new ones after the eruption.

Viola and Harry McNutt's house wasn't destroyed during the eruption. But their first floor was filled from top to bottom with hot mud from the mudflow.

The McNutts chose to keep their home near the volcano. Why, you might ask?

"We like it here," said Harry. "It's a mighty pretty place."